**Copyright © 2021**
**All rights reserved.**   part of this book may be reproduced in any form without permission from the publisher, except as permitted by U.S. copyright law. For permissions, contact: ejenterprise45@gmail.com

# HOW TO START A BUSINESS

# AS A TEEN

A Beginners Step-by-Step Guide for Starting Your Own Business as a

Teenager

## Table of Contents

INTRODUCTION ..................................................4

CHAPTER ONE ...................................................6

HOW I STARTED MY BUSINESS AS A TEEN ............6

CHAPTER TWO ................................................. 23

WHAT ARE THE CHARACTERISTICS OF A SUCCESSFUL TEEN ENTREPRENEUR? ................... 23

CHAPTER THREE ............................................. 58

CREATE YOUR BUSINESS PLAN .............................. 58

CHAPTER FOUR .............................................. 76

REGISTER YOUR BUSINESS ...................................... 76

CHAPTER FIVE ............................................. 115

OBTAIN BUSINESS PERMITS AND LICENCES .... 115

CHAPTER SIX................................................. 119

UNDERSTAND THE LAWS AND REGULATIONS IN BUSINESS ...................................................... 119

CHAPTER SEVEN .......................................................... 161

FINANCING YOUR BUSINESS ................................. 161

CHAPTER EIGHT .......................................................... 171

PAYING TAXES FOR YOUR BUSINESS.................. 171

CHAPTER NINE............................................................ 176

VARIOUS BUSINESSES YOU CAN START AS A TEEN .............................................................................. 176

CONCLUSION............................................................... 210

# INTRODUCTION

Many people are afraid of failing. Although they are aware that starting and growing a business can provide them with financial independence, they are hesitant to do so because they know some people who have failed in their endeavors. They are afraid that their fate will befall them as well. What they don't realize is that each individual is distinct.

The experiences of others may or may not be shared by him. Others' success may not be his success. Those who are successful in business have also failed in their pursuit of success, but they do not let their past failures define them. They try and try again. Life is a learning experience. People learn from their mistakes.

Reading is also a source of learning for many people. As a result, this book was written to meet the needs of aspiring entrepreneurs who want to be successful businessmen but don't know where to begin. This book's chapters are all simple to read and comprehend. Business concepts are stated clearly and concisely.

Finally, this book aims to inspire every teenager to become an entrepreneur, start a business, and succeed.

# CHAPTER ONE

# HOW I STARTED MY BUSINESS AS A TEEN

Business has always piqued my curiosity. I started manufacturing and selling bespoke T-shirts, bracelets, and soap when I was 12 years old, largely to my relatives. A few years later, my father purchased me several business/finance books, which I devoured. At that point, I decided I wanted to establish my own business. The only difficulty was that I didn't have a business plan or any money set aside.

The next section explains my experience with one of my earliest business ideas. I was 15 years old and still in school at the time. I went through various ups and downs. Nonetheless, it was an exciting period for me, and I gained a lot of new skills along the road while also earning a lot of money for a teenager. I hope this book inspires you or someone you know who is thinking about starting a business. If I could achieve it at the age of 15, you should also be able to do it.

## GENERATING A BUSINESS IDEA

After reading the books my father had purchased for me, I began to consider other business ventures. I pondered it for a few days. When I realized that I wanted to grow the business, I made the decision to do so. So I decided to create an internet business, but I had no idea what I would sell.

The obvious next step was to think about what skills or interests I have that could benefit the business. One of my passions at the time was learning magic tricks. I thought it would be fun to open an online magic shop, so I gave it a shot.

In retrospect, I didn't give the business idea any thought. I simply chose the first one I had. Now, I'd definitely think more about topics like:

- Do I have the necessary resources to put the plan into action? Can I acquire them if they aren't available?
- How quickly can I put the idea into action?
- Will I be able to profit from the idea, and if so, how?
- Is this a good time to do it?

- Is this a business idea that I'm interested in? – It's critical to keep motivated throughout the road!

## MAKE A BUSINESS PLAN

When I got a business idea, I went to my father and asked for money. He didn't offer me the money, but he did ask me to write a business plan. My first business plan was only 10 pages long after a quick internet search and some quick brainstorming. It was mostly concerned with the tasks I needed to perform to establish the online store. Among the tasks were the following:

- Decide which things I will sell.
- Determine how much of a markup I should include.
- Create a website

- Host the website and purchase a domain name
- Locate a wholesaler
- Purchase inventory or investigate dropshipping options.
- Forming a corporation is not possible at the age of 15; hence an alternative must be found.
- Determine how I will market my business.
- Establish a budget for completing all of the aforementioned tasks.

If you want to start your own business, I recommend that you prepare a business plan as well. It doesn't have to be overly detailed. The primary goal of drafting a business plan is to outline a step-by-step plan for yourself to attain your objectives. It aids with the organization of your thoughts and allows you to pinpoint any areas where you may want outside support. It should also include a budget outlining how much money you will require to establish and run your business. Finally, you should assess how much profit you can make and whether or not the business can be sustained in the future.

## FIRST TASKS COMPLETED

Once the business plan was completed, I began working on tasks requiring no financial investment. First, I discovered a coder who promised to construct a simple web store for $100. (this was in 2007). He requested a 50% down payment and a 50% payment after the work was completed. Then I contacted a few distributors worldwide and found a handful I liked. They sent me their pricing lists, and I began calculating how much the things would cost me (including shipping and import charges) and how much I could charge for them in my online store. Unfortunately, those wholesalers did not provide dropshipping and demanded full payment for new consumers. This meant that I needed a higher initial investment.

I recognized at this time that I didn't have enough money to start the business on my own. I talked to my father, and he said he could give me half of the money, but I would have to find the other half somewhere else. As a result, I began seeking a business partner.

## LOCATING A BUSINESS PARTNER AND GETTING THE BUSINESS STARTED

When you're 15, where would you look for a business partner? Other family and friends were my possibility. I chose to collaborate with a good friend who was also interested in magic tricks. We submitted our business concept to his parents, who agreed to provide us with the remaining 50% of the funds.

We built the website, purchased some minor inventory, registered a domain name, and launched our online store over the next few months. Everything was OK till that point, but we had forgotten about one thing — sales! We genuinely had no idea how or to whom we would market our products. To address the traffic and sales issues, we attempted to sell the online store to our friends, on social media, and locally in our community. We were able to sell a few things before deciding to make our business legal and form a legal entity (in our parents' names).

## THE FIRST MAJOR PROBLEM

We had originally agreed on a 70/30 share split if we formed a firm. I'd get 70% of the business because I did more preliminary work and took on more duties in the future. My friend was fine with it, and we began working on the business. However, when it came to forming the corporation, my friend's parents insisted on a 50/50 split. They persuaded my friend that we should have equal shares notwithstanding our original agreement and the division of our tasks. My 15-year-old friend followed his parents' instructions and handed me an ultimatum: 50/50 or no business. We talked for hours but couldn't come to terms with anything.

The last thing he said was, "I'm opening a new store by myself!"

I lost contact with my best friend for several years due to this fight. It was one of my first negotiations, and instead of striking a compromise, I decided to stick to our initial arrangement. At the time, I was convinced that was the proper thing to do. We both didn't know how to handle this type of issue, and it ended badly, permanently damaging our friendship.

If you ever find yourself in a position similar to this one, keep these guidelines in mind.

- If you treasure a friendship, don't let it dwindle due to a terrible bargain.

- It can be tough to combine business and friendship at times. Set hard boundaries before the negotiation if you sense any issues in a friendship due to a pending dispute.
- Keep an eye on the negotiation's temperature. When negotiation with friends begins to "hot up," look for ways to "cool off" or postpone the negotiation to another day.

## Starting from the beginning?

I was now on my own, without a business partner and with no idea what to do next. The internet magic shop was not performing well, and I was considering alternative business ventures. Needless to say, I was dissatisfied. Meanwhile, my best friend was launching a new internet magic shop.

A magician meetup that I attended a few months later was a significant turning moment. My plan was to find someone like-minded who could be interested in joining my business venture. The meetup didn't turn out the way I had hoped. I met the event's organizers, who were two professional magicians traveling the world. When I mentioned my business idea, they told me that they had always wanted to operate a local magic shop but didn't have the time. I didn't think twice and told them, "Let's do it together!"

The choice to work with these two magicians was an excellent one. I could learn a lot about the industry, and the business could expand much faster. They knew more wholesalers, the greatest things to sell, and had numerous marketing ideas. I didn't have to bother about forming a legal corporation because they already had one. Furthermore, they could supply funds to help me build the firm, which I lacked at the moment.

We set a goal of opening the business at a local shopping mall shortly before Christmas, which was only two months away.

## SUCCESS – THE OPENING OF OUR STORE

We opened our magic shop in early December of 2007. It was the holiday season, and our merchandise sold out considerably faster than anticipated. We also started making our own products, such as instructional DVDs and our own magic tricks. During the Christmas season, our daily sales averaged more than $800. It was fantastic, and I assumed we'd keep growing indefinitely.

However, once the Christmas rush was passed, sales plummeted. Then came the 2008 Financial Crisis. Talk about a dose of harsh truth. People didn't want to buy magic tricks, and we barely earned a profit during the next year. The store demanded a lot of our time but did not pay enough to keep us all engaged. That's when I decided to leave the business, put my business(es) on hold, and attend university. My business partners continued to manage the business for a while, but nothing really changed, and they eventually closed it down.

### Was it worthwhile?

As a teenager, I think it's a great idea to start a business of your own. You gain a huge advantage if you start early. You can explore concepts that will not make you millions of dollars, but you will learn a lot about entrepreneurship and prepare yourself for future challenges.

You also learn how to deal with failure, which is an inevitable part of the process. First and second attempts may not yield the results you desire; in fact, many things may go awry. The secret to overcoming failure is to never give up. Always remember to learn from your mistakes and keep going forward.

## 5 KEY TAKEAWAYS FROM BEGINNING A BUSINESS EARLY

- Simply begin; this is how you will learn. You may start a business and become an entrepreneur at any age.

- Develop a business plan. It will assist you in developing a step-by-step plan and organizing your thoughts.
- Be tenacious! You're not going to be successful right now.
- Almost all ideas at the start are lousy ideas; it is only through testing that you can arrive at a good concept.
- There will be setbacks, but they're inevitable. When the stakes are low, it is better to learn.
- Reach out to others, and don't be afraid to do so. Start-ups are thrilling because you can only get so far on your own. Making it to the finish line of a project gives you a sense of satisfaction.
- Increase your self-esteem! When you make a plan, start a business, confront many

challenges, and solve them, you are not only increasing your business but also your confidence.

- Improve your money management skills. One of the most crucial life things to learn is how money works. The sooner you get started, the better.

# CHAPTER TWO

# WHAT ARE THE CHARACTERISTICS OF A SUCCESSFUL TEEN ENTREPRENEUR?

A person who wishes to start his or her own business believes that it will be both rewarding and exciting. While doing something he enjoys, he can make a good living. He establishes his own schedule. He is the boss of himself. To be successful in business, he will need to work hard, be creative, and plan.

## A SUCCESSFUL ENTREPRENEUR'S CHARACTERISTICS AND SKILLS

An entrepreneur who succeeds must possess the appropriate skills and characteristics. He must be willing to take risks. Being his own boss is exciting, but it also requires him to make difficult decisions. The fact that he owns a business does not guarantee that he will be able to realize his ambitions. He can be an entrepreneur if he understands uncertainty and is willing to take calculated risks. A nascent entrepreneur must be prepared to make numerous decisions on his or her own. He must not be afraid of rejection. He can also rely on his instincts.

A business owner has a lot of clouts. With his ideas, he can persuade partners, potential creditors, employees, and customers. He enjoys conversing with people of various backgrounds. He easily engages other people. His arguments are supported by facts. He is also an accomplished negotiator. A small business owner must be skilled at negotiating because he must always close a deal. He must make certain that his business runs smoothly and that he saves money. An entrepreneur is also someone who is innovative in his thinking. He must devise solutions to ordinary citizens' problems. To see new opportunities, he must be able to think creatively. Before starting a business as a teen, you must ensure that you have a solid support structure. You need the support of a network of people who can help you make important decisions. You can find a mentor in business that can help you grow and succeed.

## Understand the Market

To be successful, the entrepreneur must understand the industry in which his business operates, as well as his competitors and customers. Market research is required to understand the products and services that are currently in demand so that he can plan how to compete in his chosen market. Market research reduces business risks, identifies opportunities, and identifies potential and current industry problems.

The entrepreneur must understand how to conduct proper market research. The first thing he needs to do is figure out which government agencies provide industry and market data. These government agencies are able to provide official information and data on the current state of the economy, industries, and businesses.

These records can be used by the entrepreneur in his market research. He can also get information from academic institutions, business magazines, trade groups, and other organizations that collect and analyze business data. The internet, on the other hand, is a rich supply of data. Finally, he must comprehend the international trade scene. Because of globalization, the entrepreneur must be aware of international factors that may have an impact on his business. Furthermore, he must be aware of potential international markets for his business.

**Validating Your Assumptions**

Every business concept is predicated on a set of assumptions. A business assumption is something you believe to be true about your business based on your previous experiences, but for which you do not have solid proof. A business assumption can refer to any aspect of your business plans, such as market conditions, internal expectations, or anticipated resources.

Conduct as much research as possible to eliminate assumptions and turn them into known variables. Even after you've eliminated as many assumptions as possible, you'll discover that some remain. Until you get started, there is no way to know all of the variables in your new business ventures.

Assumptions are dynamic and change as you gather more knowledge and proceed through the startup process, so keep this in mind. Do not be concerned if some of your fundamental assumptions change. When your assumptions change, it shows that you're paying attention to and taking input from your first customers into consideration.

Take a risk with your first assumptions and follow your instincts, but be sure to keep an eye out for new information and data as you go along. Most importantly, don't be afraid to change your assumptions when necessary. Make a note of all of the assumptions you've made so far and cross them off one by one. Make a list of your top five assumptions based on what you've learned so far.

[Examples of business assumptions: We can increase our market share by 5%. When our target market sees our solution, they will recognize it. We have the ability to outperform a competitor in some way or in a specific niche. Our revenue will increase at a set rate. We will be able to meet our per-unit profit projections. Step-by-step business startup guides are appealing to aspiring entrepreneurs.]

## TYPICAL EXCUSES

Every worthwhile endeavor in life has challenges that must be overcome. Consider barriers such as an entry fee or a tax that must be paid in order to participate. In the parts that follow, you'll learn about some of the frequent challenges that entrepreneurs like you face and how to overcome them. The solutions to these problems will be covered later in this guidebook.

### It's Too Difficult to Start a New Business

If it were simple, everyone would do it. Starting and running a business is difficult, but when done correctly, it is amazing and fulfilling work. As a business owner, you'll be expected to put in the time and effort to ensure that your business succeeds, and you'll be expected to help your employees and customers along the way. Those looking for an easy ride should steer clear of business ownership. Your natural genius, combined with your own unique set of skillsets and experiences, can be used to solve problems in entrepreneurship.

Though starting a business is difficult, there is guidance and resources available to help simplify those difficulties and make the process more rewarding.

**My business requires funding.**

How much money will it take to get your business off the ground? As a Fortune 500 company launches a new product or service, many people see a big launch as a sign of success. Even if you don't have Gates or

Zuckerberg's money, who wouldn't want to start a new business? In reality, when you start with fewer resources, you become more deliberate and focused on making the best use of those resources. You become more focused on outcomes, ensuring that your assumptions are correct and making adjustments quickly when they are not. Starting small allows you to maintain closer contact with your customers and better meet their needs. There is a lot less money required to start a successful new business than you might think. In order to sell to your customers, you will need to gain a better understanding of their requirements and frustrations by spending less money in the beginning to build your initial products and services and by requiring that these products and services start generating revenue.

**This provides a more stable foundation for future growth.**

Most importantly, it is far preferable to launch now, as a smaller, leaner business, rather than wait until you have amassed a war chest. Time is the most valuable resource in any business. Don't waste time waiting for better conditions or more funding. The sooner you get started, the better.

### What if My Business Fails?

Everything we do, including your current or previous job, contains varying degrees of uncertainty. Indeed, many would argue that having a traditional job is fraught with more uncertainty. A bad boss, a downturn in the economy, outsourcing to other countries, technological advances, and even a change in government policy can all result in layoffs and even the loss of positions that most people would consider "stable" or "low-risk."

Ownership gives you the freedom to make decisions that are in the best interest of everyone involved, including your employees and customers, business partners, and yourself. There will be no layoffs at all unless it is absolutely necessary. You're correct, by the way! Instead of relying on someone else's business decisions, it is preferable to take control of your own destiny. Taking action is preferable to having one's actions taken for you.

Consider whether or not the risk of starting your own business outweighs the risk of working for someone else. Your decisions, preparation, course corrections, and the formation of a strong team capable of overcoming any obstacle are all ways in which you can reduce the risks associated with running a business.

## The development of a perfect product is too time-consuming and expensive

If you have a product that does what you say it does, it doesn't matter how excellent it is. If you develop too much, you risk not delivering your product or service to customers, and if you do not develop enough, your business will fail. To achieve that perfect balance, the product should be able to solve the customer's problem the vast majority of the time, with only a few instances of failure or disappointment. We didn't say there would be no failures or disappointments. If your product or service can achieve those types of results, you are ready to launch, even if some tweaking could be done to improve the product.

Consider any major corporation or product brand. They release a product that does something amazing once a year. The following year, they released the same product with a few new improvements. The product may be re-released the following year with changes to the scope of what it can do. The minimal viable product model, popularized by Eric Ries, is followed by a business that employs this type of product development strategy. The basic idea is to create a product that delivers the results it promises and nothing more, then release it into the market, then improve the product based on market feedback. As a result, you save time and money developing the product or service and can get a better idea of how well it will perform in the market sooner.

How do you know if your product or service is minimally viable? An initial prototype must be built. A prototype is a testable preliminary model of your product or service. If the prototype is capable of producing the desired results, it can be copied. If the prototype fails to produce the desired results, it must be modified until it does. Prototypes can be created relatively cheaply, depending on the complexity of your product or service.

We had a business idea a few years ago that involved the production of a product. Before incurring the expense of full-fledged manufacturing, we created the product out of wood. We created an injection-molded prototype after resolving the issues with the wood prototype. Finally, we invested in the development of a blow mold for the product and began mass production. This progression allowed us to step through the testing process methodically, avoiding costly mistakes in design, functionality, and aesthetics.

Once you've created a prototype, it's time to start testing. While having people in your network test your product is a good place to start, if your testing consists of grandma, your neighbor, and your best friend, you will need to do some additional testing. Sending surveys to people you know in your target market will also help your testing process.

Product reviews from members of your well-defined target market should be the focus of your product research for greater effectiveness. Consider putting together a test group or focus group and asking specific questions about your product or service, their potential interest in purchasing it, how much they are willing to pay, what they like or dislike, what features or benefits are most important to them, and so on. Your focus group should test your product or service in real-world scenarios and report on their level of satisfaction. The feedback from this group can be invaluable if you carefully select willing participants from a well-defined target market.

Businesses that only provide a service rather than a tangible product frequently overlook the importance of testing. If your service does not produce the desired results for your customer, it is as valuable as an electronic device that does not turn on (a highly-priced paperweight). For your service-based business, do not overlook the testing phase. In exchange for valuable feedback, offer a free or reduced-price trial of your service. Put your service through a stress test with a focus group. What happens if everything goes wrong with your service? A small investment in testing now can save you a lot of time and money later.

After thoroughly testing your idea in your ideal target market, consider reaching out to your niche or target market in different geographical areas to see if your product or service has the same level of reception or appeal and if any additional improvements or adjustments are required. This type of multi-regional testing may indicate a future opportunity to grow or scale your business.

What are some methods for testing your product or service? How can you question your assumptions and look at your product or service from a different angle?

**Discovering Your Purpose and Passion for What You Do**

Your passion and purpose are the "x-factors" that will make or break your new business as you launch and operate it. Knowing your true passions will help you reduce risk and ensure your success as a new business owner. Passion is the fuel that will propel your business forward, even when times are tough, and if your business is not an extension of your personal passion and purpose, its development will be difficult and draining. You will find success and fulfillment as you harness and focus your personal passion on providing valuable solutions to the problem your target market is experiencing, and the money will follow as a byproduct of your efforts.

As a person, you have gathered a wealth of unique qualities and experiences throughout the course of your life that make you uniquely qualified to pursue your passion. It is the combination of these factors that distinguishes you as uniquely qualified to serve your customers. Your business requires its own mission statement. That purpose should be heavily influenced by your own personal passion and purpose, as well as the passions and purposes of any business partners you may have. However, assuming that everyone in your business understands and agrees with your purpose and passion is not enough. Your business must have a defined purpose that will act as the glue that holds all of your business partners and employees together, allowing them to work as one to accomplish far more than any single person is capable of accomplishing on their own.

Write down your business' passion and purpose and place them in a prominent location where they will be seen frequently. Becoming re-acquainted with the reasons you got into a business in the first place will help you stay on track.

Every aspect of your business should be influenced by its mission. Your goals, focus, annual objectives, and three-year plan should all revolve around the passion and purpose you've defined for your business. While all of those business elements may change and evolve as your business grows, the purpose behind them should remain steadfast, strong, and constant.

As an example, your company's mission statement is "to assist aspiring entrepreneurs in succeeding." It's possible your offerings and methods for assisting aspiring business owners will evolve over time, but your core mission will not. Your annual production goals, the number of customers you assist each month, and even your revenue goals may change and grow over time, but your purpose will never change. You exist "to assist aspiring entrepreneurs in succeeding."

What is the goal of your business? What will it do, and what justifies its existence? What is the primary advantage you will provide to your customers? List your goal.

_____

_____

_____

Do you already possess the drive and knowledge necessary to transform your idea into a successful business and a fulfilling way of life?

Yes ☐

No ☐

List the top three reasons you are passionate about your solution.

_____

_____

_____

List the skills, talents, and abilities you or your partners possess that lead to your business passion:

_____

_____

_____

List the skills, talents, or abilities you want or need to develop to be successful in business: (Are any of these skills or abilities you could learn from a business advisor?)

_____

_____

_____

Why will your customers see you as an expert in your field?

**A Mission for Your Purpose**

Your mission, unlike your purpose, is likely to change as your business grows and develops. A business mission is defined as a mission statement, which is a formal summary of the business' values and goals. Everyone on your staff should be able to read and understand the three- to three-and-a-half- to three-year goals of your business. It should be specific in describing what "mission accomplished" means at the end of that time frame.

Many people mix up their mission and purpose. The purpose of a business does not change and is intended to be a guide for the entire life of the business, whereas a mission statement is effective for a specific time frame and then is updated after that time frame elapses. There will be a new mission statement written for the next three years after you've met your three-year goals.

What will your mission statement include? For example, how many customers will you have served after one, two, and three years of operation? What are your projected annual revenues at the end of your mission statement period? Your mission statement should be directly related to your purpose and should include revenue or profit center goals. How many workers will you have?

How many units will you sell in the first, second, and third years of your mission statement's timeframe? What growth metrics are you going to track and work to improve? What are your thoughts on the initial mission statement for your company? What goals do you hope to achieve in the next 1-3 years? How will you fulfill your mission while also generating revenue? Fill in the blanks with your mission statement:

_____

## MANTRA: THE SIMPLE STATEMENT ABOUT WHAT YOUR BUSINESS WILL ACTUALLY DO

Guy Kawasaki argues in his book "The Art of the Start" that your mantra should be 2-4 words long and should succinctly describe what you do. This is similar to a mission statement but much shorter. Here are some fictitious mantras for well-known companies: 'Better than driving,' says Southwest Airlines. 'Stop suffering,' says the Red Cross. 'Bring people together,' says the United Way. 'Kick butt in the air and space,' says the US Air Force.

After you've launched, you should be able to ask anyone associated with your business, "What does our company do for our customers?" and they should all be able to answer the same question consistently. Your mantra is that answer what you do in 2-4 words. It should not be clever but rather simple and straightforward. For example, our mission statement is "HELPING ENTREPRENEURS LAUNCH."

I'd like to know what you've got in store for your customers. Make your own mantra suggestions by filling in the blanks:

_____

**Scalability—How Big Will Your Business Grow?**

It is critical to be clear and intentional about your desired growth and future expansion goals for your new business early in the planning process. In what capacity do you envision your business? Do you want a small mom-and-pop business to pass down to your children, or do you want to someday own a multinational corporation? The processes you implement now can either make your business "scalable" or limit it.

A business process, also known as a business system, is a set of interconnected tasks that must be completed in order to provide a good or service to the end-user or customer. A scalable business process is one that can handle increasing workload demands. When tested with ever-increasing demands, a business process or system that scales well will be able to maintain or even improve its performance and efficiency.

It may appear obvious that a business with a million customers will perform better than a business with a hundred customers, but this is not always the case. When trying to keep a million customers happy, a business that can provide excellent customer service to a hundred customers may give up. A business that can produce a hundred widgets per month may fail if there is a demand for a thousand.

As a small business grows, it is not uncommon for it to struggle and eventually fail. One example of this type of business is an ice cream stand at a farmer's market. The owner of this ice cream stand used all-natural ingredients to make the creamiest, tastiest ice cream in the world. He was very popular among the locals, and he made ice cream as quickly as he could. One day, an Oprah show representative happened upon this ice cream stand and tried a sample. She was so taken with the ice cream that she offered the owner a once-in-a-lifetime opportunity. If you were to be featured on the Oprah show, how would you like it? She inquired.

The opportunity astounded the owner. With just one of these shows, he could become an overnight national success. Then he realized his business systems were not scalable. He couldn't possibly make that much ice cream in that short amount of time. His business processes, which were designed to serve several hundred customers each day at the farmer's market, were not scalable enough to handle the thousands of orders he would likely receive after appearing on Oprah. He was powerless to turn down the offer.

Your ideal business will always be small, but when designing the systems that will run it, keep these questions in mind. Will this system now meet the needs of my business? Will it meet the needs of my business once it has grown to the size I want it to be?

What would happen if the system's demands were suddenly doubled or tripled? Will the system be able to handle the increases, or will it collapse?

Remember that your business's ultimate scalability should be aligned with the purpose you previously defined, just as your mission, goals, and mantra should be aligned with your business's stated purpose. Your mission, mantra, and system scalability can all be tweaked based on various factors and market conditions, but your purpose should not.

**Developing an Exit Strategy**

When you think about starting and running your own business, it's difficult to imagine ever wanting to sell it and move on to the next chapter of your life. The reality is that the majority of successful businesses are eventually sold, and the small percentage that is not sold is passed down to the next generation.

It's similar to purchasing a car. We tend to forget about what will happen when we have to trade in our old automobile for a new one as soon as we get our hands on the car. You might not consider keeping a maintenance log or covering the floors with mats. The value of your car will rise if you perform these two simple tasks while it is in good condition.

In the same way, when you start a new business, you never think about quitting it, but you will. Consult with an expert who has experience in exit strategy planning and begin thinking about your exit strategy as soon as possible. Take the essential actions early in the process to ensure that your firm is ready for sale or transfer when the time comes.

# CHAPTER THREE

# CREATE YOUR BUSINESS PLAN

The business plan is a map that shows the direction the business will take. It is a document that contains three to five years of business planning. It also outlines how the business intends to increase its revenue.

**Executive Summary**

One of the most important parts of the business plan is the Executive Summary. In a nutshell, the reader will learn about the business, its location, its future plans, and the reasons why the business will succeed. When an entrepreneur is looking for a financier or applying for a loan, the executive summary can catch the attention of the investor. The Executive Summary highlights the business' strengths. As a result, it is frequently the last section of a business plan that the entrepreneur writes. It is, however, the first section of the document.

For a well-established business, the Executive Summary must include the mission statement, brief company information, growth highlights, products and services, financial information, and future plans. The Executive Summary should be brief and to the point. The Executive Summary for a new business or startup should focus on the entrepreneur's background and experience, as well as why he decided to start the business. It must explain how market research was conducted and why the target market requires the company's products and services.

The reader must be persuaded that the business will succeed. It must also include any future plans that the business may have.

## THE SIX MOST IMPORTANT SECTIONS OF AN EXECUTIVE SUMMARY

### Mission Statement

A brief description of your company's mission. It should be no more than a few sentences long. (This is the "mission" you mentioned in the preceding section.)

### Information about the Company

There is information here about who will be in charge and what their roles will be when the business is launched. If you are looking for business loans or investment capital, you should include a summary of these key individuals' qualifications, work experience, and past performances/success, as well as what percentage of the business each individual owns.

In this section, you should also include the business name, legal entity type (for example, S or C corporation, sole proprietorship, partnership, limited liability partnership, etc.), whether the business is privately held or publicly traded, the date the business launched (or will launch), the locations of your offices/facilities, and what your business sells in which demographic or market.

Products/Services: Describe briefly the products or services offered by the business, how those products and services will be sold, how revenue will be generated from the sale of these products or services, and any other critical information specific to those products or services.

Growth Expectations/Highlights: Highlight the expected growth of the business. There are occasions when a visual depiction, such as a graph or chart, is beneficial. Make certain that your growth projections are reasonable and grounded in as much fact as possible. A case study summary of a similar business that has met the growth projections you claim could be a useful addition.

Financial Information: Describe the cash resources available to the business right now, as well as any loans or investment capital required. Also, summarize the business's potential or realized profitability from the sale of its products/services minus the cost of producing and supporting those products/services.

Plans for the future: Describe what the company's future will look like. What are your plans for the business? What kind of success will the business have? As you paint a vision for the future of your important work, be bold in your ambitions, but keep everything realistic and achievable.

Let's get into the meat of the business plan now.

**Company Description**

The following section is the Company Description, which includes information about the various aspects of the business. It assists potential investors and readers in understanding the company's goals and unique selling proposition. The Company Description describes the company as well as its target market. It describes how the company will meet the needs of its target market. It also includes a list of businesses, organizations, and customers that the company serves or would like to serve. Finally, it explains the company's competitive advantages such as value proposition, efficient operation, expert personnel, and location.

## SWOT (Strengths, Weaknesses, Opportunities, Threats)

A SWOT analysis examines your company's internal strengths as well as external opportunities and threats. By regularly scrutinizing these four critical categories, you will be better able to identify the specific courses of action required to establish a successful business.

A key team member with extensive industry experience is an example of strength. You may discover that weakness in your company is the location of your facilities, a product flaw, or a lack of expertise in a particular area. Current trends or market forces that you will be able to exploit are an example of an opportunity. A threat could be an increase in fuel prices or new rules and regulations that impact your profitability. Threats, in general, are things that are beyond your control and are external to your company.

After you've investigated these four categories, decide how your company will handle each issue.

How will you use your key team members' experience to propel your company forward? What are your plans to make reaching your target market easier if your facilities are in a bad location and they will have difficulty finding you? Can you find a way to avoid increased costs or new regulations while still remaining profitable?

It is through answering these questions that your business model, marketing strategy, and overall business direction will be clarified. Conduct your first SWOT analysis for your company. Make a list of all the strengths, weaknesses, opportunities, and threats you can think of.

Strengths:_____

Weaknesses:_____

Opportunities:_____

Threats:_____


Items that should have been completed during day 1:

- Assumptions
- Company Purpose
- Company Mission
- Company Mantra
- Scalability Determination
- Exit Strategy Consideration
- Company Information
- SWOT Analysis


Notes and Ideas:

_____


**Market Analysis**

The Market Analysis section follows, and it illustrates market knowledge, industry, research findings, and conclusions. In this section, the entrepreneur must include the business's outlook and industry description, target market information, distinguishing characteristics of the target market; target market size; the market share percentage the company wishes to gain; gross margin and pricing targets; competitor analysis; and regulatory restrictions.

**Management and Organization**

Following the Market Analysis, the Organization and Management section includes the company's organizational structure. It also includes information about its ownership, the management team's profiles, and the board members' qualifications. It is critical to include each member of management's job description. Benefits and salaries, as well as levels of advancement, are also discussed.

**Goods and Services**

The product or service line is the next section of the business plan. It describes the product or service that the company provides or wishes to provide. The entrepreneur discusses the benefits of his service or product to his target market in this section. It also includes information about the product or service's life cycle, as well as any pending, anticipated, or existing patent or copyright filings. Finally, in this section, outline the research and development activities.

**Sales and marketing**

The following section is about the Marketing and Sales Strategy. Customers can only be gained and retained through a business's marketing efforts. The marketing strategy must be defined clearly. Although there are numerous approaches to developing a marketing strategy, the entrepreneur's strategy must be unique to his business and must be evaluated on a regular basis. A marketing strategy may include a communication strategy, a distribution channel strategy, a growth strategy, or a market penetration strategy. The growth strategy includes a vertical strategy in which the entrepreneur offers the same products and services at different distribution levels. Retailers, distributors, internal sales forces, and original equipment manufacturers are examples of distribution channels. Flyers, catalogs, brochures, personal selling, public relations, advertising, and promotions are all part of the communication strategy.

The overall sales strategy must be defined after the marketing strategy. It must contain a sales force strategy as well as sales activities. The salesforce strategy includes salesperson recruitment, recruitment strategies, salesperson training, and sales force compensation. Identifying potential customers, the number of sales calls made over time, and the average number of calls per sale, average dollar amount per vendor, and average dollar amount per sale are all part of the sales activities.

**Funding Request**

The Funding Request section comes next. This section is critical for the entrepreneur if he is looking for funding for his business. It includes the amount of money his business currently requires, the funds he requires over the next five years, how the money will be used, and any future financial plans such as selling the business, debt repayment, acquisition, or buyout.

**Financial Projections**

The Financial Projections section follows. This section aims to efficiently allocate resources after the market has been analyzed and objectives have been established. If the company is already established, this section must include historical data on the company's performance. Creditors want to see at least three years of financial performance history. For each year of business operation, the entrepreneur must include cash flow statements, balance sheets, and income statements. Creditors will also be interested in the collateral that the entrepreneur can offer in exchange for the loan. All businesses must include prospective financial data in their business plans. Creditors want to know how the entrepreneur intends to expand the business over the next five years. Financial statements that have been forecasted must be presented. If the company is new, financial projections must be provided monthly or quarterly. The entrepreneur can present yearly or quarterly projections for the coming years.

**Appendix**

A business plan's appendix contains additional information that isn't included in the main document but may be helpful to the reader. The appendix can include the business's and the entrepreneur's credit history, resumes of members of the management team, product pictures, letters of reference, market study results, relevant book references or magazine articles, licenses and permits, patents (if any), copies of leases, legal documents, building permits, a list of business consultants, and contracts. The distribution of business plans must be recorded and controlled in order to facilitate updating and monitoring.

For the entrepreneur's business plan to stand out, he must make an effort. The reader must have a clear understanding of the nature of the business and how the entrepreneur intends to make it successful. The entrepreneur must provide a detailed description of his goods and services. He must have a clear plan for making his business stand out. He must have a plan in place for selling his products and services to his target market. By offering specialized products and services, most small businesses cater to a specific market niche. It is also critical that the entrepreneur understands his market niche. He can identify his own niche by using his market knowledge or conducting a market survey.

# CHAPTER FOUR

# REGISTER YOUR BUSINESS

To begin a business, a business name must first be chosen and registered. The company cannot apply for government funding unless it is registered.

**Registering Your Business Name**

To register a business name, many new entrepreneurs must also register a "Doing Business As" (DBA) name. It is not the same as incorporation. It does not include trademark protection. It means that an entrepreneur is letting the state know that he is doing business by using a name other than his own. Using a "Doing Business As" name indicates that a corporation or partnership is doing business under a different name than its legal one. He can also apply for a trademark for his company name and logo.

A "Doing Business As" name is a name that differs from the registered name of the business. It is also distinct from the names of the partners or the personal name of the entrepreneur. In the United States of America, the entity or entrepreneur's name is the default name of the business. If the individual registers a "Doing Business As" name, he can change it. If the sole proprietor or partners want to use a business name other than their own, a DBA name is required.

It is also required if the limited liability company or corporation is already in operation and the shareholders want to change the name of the company. The DBA name is registered with the state government or the county clerk's office. There are, however, some states that do not require DBA registration.

A partnership, limited liability company, nonprofit organization, or corporation must register with the state government. A sole proprietorship does not necessitate a state registration. However, sole proprietors must register their business if they wish to operate it under a different name. Even if a business is already in operation, it is possible to change its type. On its website, the Internal Revenue Service has procedures for changing the business structure.

**Choose Your Business Name**

It's practically easy and straightforward choosing a name for your business because you may have been dreaming about the name since you were five years old, or it can be extremely frustrating and time-consuming as you constantly try to discover the perfect but elusive name, or it can be anywhere in between. You will need a name that is available in the state(s) where your business will be registered, as well as a name that is available online as a URL that ends in.com or.org if possible.

According to Murphy's law, you will most likely have a moment of extreme inspiration only to discover that 26 other companies have already used that exact name (or a very similar variation) and that the URL has already been registered.

If you give it enough time, the process of choosing a name can be enjoyable and inspiring. When you start to get frustrated with the process and can't seem to come up with the perfect name, take a break and let your subconscious mind take over for a little while. Take a power nap, sleep on it overnight, or come back to it later in the day when you can approach it with a fresh perspective. In the end, the name you choose is less important than how closely you adhere to your purpose and mission and how well you solve problems for your customers.

The name of your business will not make or break your success, but a bad name can stymie your progress and success if, for example, it is difficult for your customers to associate the name you choose with what your business does, or if the name you choose is difficult to remember or understand. A good marketing plan, on the other hand, can often overcome the problems associated with a bad name. To help you choose the right name, here are some tips:

**Be creative and make something up.**

Professional naming firms created the names Acura and Compaq. In their names, they both use root words that convey a feature or benefit of their products or businesses. Acura, for example, means "precise" in many different languages, and Compaq was derived from combining compatibility and quality. Using a made-up name will make it easier to find a matching URL; just make sure the name is easy to pronounce and has no negative connotations.

**Use your own name or a variation of it.**

A bit of your name can help you come up with an original business name that isn't already taken. You may benefit from this if you have a unique first or last name. Perhaps add a portion of your name to the type of business or industry in which you operate, or experiment with combinations of your name and descriptions of what you do. Instead of using your own name, a combination of the name of a city, county, state, or a well-known landmark near where you will operate your business and a description of what your business does may be the perfect combination. For example, Mark Lundenburg's company could be called "Lundeberg Printing," while Richard Smith's company could be called "Rich Financial Services," and Jake from Denver, Colorado could be called "Mile-high Washers."

**Avoid negative connotations.**

Dentists, doctors, and lawyers frequently use their personal names as part of their business names; however, Dr. James Youngblood should probably avoid using the "Youngblood" part of his name for a pediatric dental practice due to the negative connotation associated with blood and dentistry. Perhaps "Dr. Jim The Dentist" would be a better name for pediatric dentistry (sorry, James). Focus on how the names could be misread or misconstrued when you have a selection of business names.

**Keep it concise and descriptive.**

The name should be short enough to be easily remembered while also descriptive enough to indicate what the business does from the name. "Mic

Howell and Sons Custom Curb Address Painting" is a descriptive business name, but it might be too long to remember. "Addresses On Curbs" is less difficult to say while still being descriptive enough for anyone to understand what the company does.

**Make it simple to read.**

An easy-to-read business name is easy to spell and pronounce. Obscure spellings can make your name difficult to pronounce and, as a result, remember. How do you say the name "Nvidia"? Would you pronounce it NAII-vid-ee-a, un-VID-ee-a, or ne-VID-ee-ah? This electronics manufacturer says it en-VID-ee-ah. What about the sportswear manufacturer Adidas? Most Americans pronounce it ah-DEE-das, which has stuck, but the correct pronunciation is AH-di-das. Both of these companies have accepted the widespread mispronunciation of their names and have overcome the difficulty through numerous costly advertising campaigns. In your new business, it will be much easier and less expensive to advertise a name that is simple to spell and pronounce.

**Avoid using initials and acronyms.**

Avoid using acronyms and initials in the early stages of your new business. Companies such as 3M and KFC did not begin with those names. Both KFC and 3M were previously named as the Minnesota Mining and Manufacturing Company and Kentucky Fried Chicken, respectively. Their names were later abbreviated after the businesses had penetrated the initial markets they pursued and decided to expand into new markets. Consider using a descriptive name that can be shortened as you gain more traction if necessary.

TIP: A dedicated brainstorming session is a good way to come up with solid business name options. Narrow down your top 5 or 10 best business names, and then ask a few people who are definitely in your target market to pick their top 2. Always place a higher value on the opinions of your target market than on the opinions of people with whom you regularly socialize. If a name resonates and connects with people who are clearly within your target market, it is most likely a good name for your company. Consider repurposing those business names on your shortlist that didn't make the final cut to become the names of products, offerings, special programs, or services you provide to your customers.

List your top 10 choices for business names.

1._____

2._____

3._____

4._____

5._____

6._____

7._____

8._____

9._____

10._____

Have at least 5 people who would be members of your niche review those names and circle their favorites above.

## Website Hosting and URL Availability

www.bluehost.com, www.godaddy.com, and www.hostgator.com are three popular domain registrars. All of these services will allow you to conduct a quick search of available URLs (also known as domain names) to see if your company name is also available to be the name of your website. Bluehost is recommended because it has a solid control panel (cPanel) that allows you to change aspects of your website hosting using a graphical interface. They also have excellent customer service and provide unlimited hosting space when you buy multiple domain names.

Bluehost's services are used by us, and we have an affiliate relationship with them (full disclosure). Bluehost is ideal for startups because it offers numerous options for expanding your online presence as your business grows. A dedicated server option is available if your site receives large volumes of traffic or if something on your site goes viral, allowing you to handle much more traffic without your site crashing.

www.com is a website that performs a quick and easy search for URL availability. If you enter your preferred name into the search field on this site, it will return possible domain names that are similar to your business name as well as alternatives if your preferred name is not available. One advantage of beginning your domain search at Domain rather than other sites that sell domain names is that Domain does not have advertisements or a complicated layout that may distract you from your task. When you've found a URL that works well for your company on Domain, you can go to your preferred hosting provider and secure the name.

If you can't find a business name that can also be a URL, consider using an abbreviation of your company name as a URL. For example, if your company name is Doodle Lectures and you want to allow professors to draw illustrations as part of their lectures and distribute those drawings digitally to their students, but www.doodlelectures.com is not available, you could consider shortening your URL to www.doodlelect.com. Shortening your URL is rarely optimal, but it is necessary when other options are unavailable.

When you've determined that your preferred business name is available online, go ahead and register the domain URL with the registrar whose hosting service you'll be using. It is inconvenient to register the Domain with one registrar and then transfer it to another, so choose a registrar and stick with them. The cost of registering your URL will typically range from $5 to $100 per year/per Domain, depending on the registrar you use. If you find an available URL, especially one that ends in the coveted ".com" suffix, you should act quickly to register it.

Which of your top ten business names would work well as a URL?

_____

_____

_____

_____

_____


Which hosting service will you register your domain name (URL) with?

_____

**Check Name Availability with Your State Government**

All states have websites where you can search for available business names and those currently in use. Search for "(your state name) business entity search" and scroll through the results to find the dedicated business name search site for your state.

Most state business name search websites will then have a search field where you can enter your proposed business name, and the search will return a list of company names that are similar to the name you searched for. If your state's system is not accommodating, you can use one of several online third-party "business name availability" sites. Use your state's website as our primary source of the most accurate and up-to-date information whenever possible.

TIP: Before you worry about registering your preferred business name with your state, see if it is available as a URL. It is frequently more difficult to locate an available URL than it is to locate an available business name with the state. Even if the state does not have the name of your choice, you may typically make a minor change to it so that you can use it. For example, "www.prohair-care.com" could be the ideal URL for you. If the state has already taken that name, you could register as "The Pro Hair Care Company," "Pro Hair Care, LLC," or "Pro Hair Care Etc." and still use the same URL.

We'll lead you through the process of starting a business in the state where it will be situated in the next section. If you are not yet ready to organize or incorporate your business, most states will allow you to reserve the business name through a streamlined business registration process. This registration process basically locks up the name and makes it impossible for someone else to use that name for a different business even if you have not formally organized or incorporated your legal entity for a small fee that varies by state.

Things that should have been done:

- Make a shortlist of possible names for your company.
- Created a business URL.
- Determined the availability of names in your state.

**Notes and Ideas:**

_____

_____

_____

_____

**EIN (Employer Identification Number)**

For most federal entities, an EIN (Employer Identification Number) is a number assigned by the Internal Revenue Service (IRS). Basically, it's like a social security number in that way. This is also known as a Tax Identification Number (or Tax ID) or a Federal Employer Identification Number (or FEIN). Some states require you to provide an EIN when forming an LLC or incorporating your business, and most banks require it when opening a business banking account, a merchant account to accept credit card payments, or when paying yourself a salary. As the name implies, you will undoubtedly use the Employer Identification Number when you are ready to hire employees and whenever you file any employee-related forms. Because you will need your EIN frequently, keep it in a safe place where you can easily access it.

If the kind of business you want to run is a sole proprietorship, you can use your personal Social Security number as your EIN until you hire employees, start a retirement plan, buy or inherit an existing company, file bankruptcy, or change your business structure to something other than a sole proprietorship. Even if you are the sole employee of your company, you will still require an EIN unless you are a sole proprietorship. Because an EIN is used for so many things, we recommend that you get one even if you are not required to have one.

You can apply for an EIN in a variety of ways, which are detailed on the IRS "How to Apply for an EIN" page. The IRS "Internet EIN" portal is the preferred application method, as the EIN is issued immediately.

Make certain that the information you submit is correct, as errors can result in time-consuming delays down the road. The EIN you receive is a critical number, so keep copies of all documentation in your corporate book and double- and triple-check for accuracy. Contact the IRS right away to correct any incorrect information.

If dealing with the IRS sounds like a hassle, and you'd rather spend your time focusing on other aspects of starting your business, our "Done For You" creation services include applying for and obtaining an EIN on your behalf.

**Request an EIN from the IRS. Fill in your EIN here for easy reference.**
**Getting Registered with the State**

Most states allow you to register your new business by visiting your state's website. You should probably register your business in the state where you live; however, if you want your business to be headquartered in Nevada, Delaware, or another state for reasons you may have heard about on the radio, you can do so; however, contact us first to learn about the pitfalls of registering in those "business-friendly" states and the costs associated with those registrations. Despite the fact that some states offer businesses a host of advantages, in the vast majority of cases, it is better to form your business in the state where you reside.

TIP: Keep your business registration simple by registering it to "live" (or be headquartered) in the same state where you live and do the majority of your business. This allows you to designate yourself as your company's registered agent, saving you money and time in the long run.

There is a greater chance that your registration will be more complicated if you plan to have physical offices or operations across multiple states or in a state where you are not a resident. Using a third-party registration agent may be necessary for these situations. A registration agent will have the necessary contacts in each state and will be able to register your business in each state quickly and correctly, despite differing state regulations.

**Requirements of the City, County, and Other States**

You will need to determine which licenses or special permits are required at the state and local levels in order to legally start and operate your business. Most small businesses will most likely only require a business license obtained from your city or county. However, special permits, approvals, and registrations are required for certain types of businesses. There are typically fewer online resources for this type of information, and determining all of the licenses you require may necessitate several phone calls or visits to local government offices.

Here is a list of typical local requirements that you will almost certainly need to meet before you can begin doing business:

- If you intend to hire employees, you must contact your state's employment division to obtain a tax withholding certificate and register with the unemployment agency.

- If you have employees, you'll also need workers' compensation insurance. For this type of insurance, most commercial insurance companies can provide a quote.

- If you intend to sell a product, you must obtain a sales and use tax certificate. Most states have online resources that will walk you through the process of obtaining the necessary registration certificates to get you started.

- Some city and county governments also require you to obtain sales and use tax certificates.

- The city or county where your business is based will require you to obtain a business license if you plan to operate out of a location other than your home.

- For personal property tax and future assessments, you may need to register with the city or county. When applicable, this personal property tax is a tax imposed and collected by the local government. Don't be misled by the term "personal"—it is a tax on property owned by the business, which generally includes furniture, fixtures, office equipment, industrial equipment, machinery, tools, supplies, inventory, and other non-real property (such as a building and the land the building is standing on). Contact your local taxation department or agency to find out what your company's personal property tax requirements are.

**Personal Asset Protection**

Protecting your personal assets begins with the proper formation of your company and continues throughout its operational life. The formation of your LLC or corporation is the first step toward self-protection. The way you run and manage your business will either maintain or erode your personal liability protection.

**TIP**: Remember that protecting your personal assets is one of your most important considerations in everything you do—it is the primary reason why you are operating your business activities through a legal entity rather than as a sole proprietorship. Make certain that your company's activities do not have a negative impact on your personal assets.

It's also a good idea to make resolutions whenever you're in charge of making major business decisions or doing anything personally related to the business. A business resolution is a document that records and formalizes a company's actions. It calls out the name of the company, the date, the parties involved, the action to be taken, the reason for the action, and the authority to take such action in its most basic form.

The resolution should define the authority the company gives you to make decisions that the company will then be bound by as the company's "Managing Member" or President. It is generally a good idea to draft an initial resolution, dated and notarized, defining the authority assigned to you very early in the process of establishing your business and before you begin doing any business.

To protect your personal assets, memorialize the important business actions. For example, if you deposit money into the company account, create a document outlining the capital investment and how it will be used. Create a business resolution stating that the company authorizes you to legally bind the company by signing a lease or contract if you are legally binding the company by signing a contract or lease.

Not every decision must be documented with a resolution; in general, written resolutions are only required for larger actions and decisions. Use your best judgment and make resolutions whenever you can imagine someone asking, "Did this decision benefit you personally more than it did the business?" Here are some more pointers to help you keep your personal and business activities separate so you can avoid activities that would "pierce the corporate veil" and destroy the liability protection provided by your legal business entity:

- Never combine your personal and business funds. Always keep your business funds in a separate bank account.
- Keep separate credit card accounts for business. Open a credit card account in the company's name to be used solely for business-related purchases, and never use your personal credit card for a business purchase.

- Every time you give cash to your company, be very deliberate about recording those cash deposits in your company ledger and indicating that they are investments. If you withdraw funds from the company for personal use or to reimburse yourself for company expenses, make sure to detail those transactions in your company ledgers. Include a statement with each transaction that explains why and for what purpose the transaction occurred.

- Never deposit a personal cash investment into the company as well as revenue generated from company sales on the same deposit slip. Keep different transaction types on separate deposit slips to keep your ledger books clean and easy to read. Despite the fact that it appears to be an unnecessary step, it will not only make it easier for you to see your profits and investments later, but it will also protect your personal assets from litigation if you consistently follow this rule.

- If you decide that the company should pay certain expenses, such as automobile lease payments, auto insurance premiums, or health insurance premiums, keep careful and detailed records of those payments separate and distinct from your personal financial records so that those payments can be easily recorded in the company books and receive proper tax treatment by your accountant or bookkeeper at tax time.

TIP: In all things financial and operational, always treat the company as a separate and distinct legal entity.


**Liability Insurance**

Aside from choosing an entity type that will provide you with some personal separation from your business's liability, another important way to reduce the risk for both your business and yourself is to obtain liability insurance. Typically, liability insurance will protect your company from losses caused by theft, property damage, bodily injury, natural disasters, legal claims, or judgments. Almost every major insurance company has a division dedicated to writing commercial liability insurance. Speak with your personal insurance agent (if you have one) about obtaining a commercial liability policy for your company. The premium will differ depending on the type of business you start.

Obtaining a business liability insurance policy should be higher on your list of priorities for some startups than for others, but it should be on your list of priorities regardless. For example, if your company manufactures or imports toys, you should have a liability policy in place before you begin selling because one mishap with one of your toys could result in a lawsuit that could bankrupt your entire company and even you personally. In general, having liability insurance in place before your company begins any business transactions is a good idea, but if your business is particularly prone to lawsuits, you may want to have liability insurance in place before even launching your new business.

The laws and requirements for business liability insurance differ depending on where you live and what industry you work in. Always seek the advice of an attorney or a CPA if you have any doubts about whether your actions are legal or tax-compliant, as well as protecting your own interests.

TIP: Spend some time shopping around and comparing the prices of a few different commercial insurance carriers. Some companies, like your personal auto insurance and most things in life, are simply less expensive while still providing comparable quality. As a startup, save your money wherever you can. In a typical business, every dollar saved on expenses can translate into $4-$5 in sales revenue. While lowering the cost of a liability insurance policy is a good way to cut startup costs, do not do so if it means sacrificing coverage. Always keep your expenses under control and your liability in mind.

When will you obtain liability insurance for your business? _____

From which insurance company will you obtain the insurance? _____

Items that should have been completed include: • Choosing the entity type for your company.

- File a tax return with the IRS.
- Get an EIN.
- Submit Articles of Incorporation and register with the state.

- Determine which licenses and permits are required, and then obtain them from your state and local governments.
- Decide when you will obtain liability insurance for your business and shop around for the best providers and prices.

# CHAPTER FIVE

# OBTAIN BUSINESS PERMITS AND LICENCES

Even if the business is small, the entrepreneur must obtain the necessary permits and licenses to operate it legally. A federal permit or license is required if the business will be involved in federally regulated and supervised activities such as commercial fishing, firearms, selling alcohol, and so on. The entrepreneur must obtain a permit from the US Department of Agriculture if the business involves the transport or import of plants, biotechnology, biologics, animal products, or animals.

Alcohol beverages must be sold, imported, wholesaled, or manufactured with a federal permit from the US Treasury's Alcohol and Tobacco Tax and Trade Bureau. In addition, the company must obtain a local business permit from the Alcohol Beverage Control Board. Certificates and licenses from the Federal Aviation Administration are required if the business involves aircraft operation, air transport of people or goods, or aircraft maintenance. A company that imports sells, or manufactures explosives, ammunition, or firearms must be licensed by the Bureau of Alcohol, Tobacco, Firearms, and Explosives.

If the entrepreneur's business involves wildlife, he or she must apply for a permit from the US Fish and Wildlife Service. If it intends to fish commercially, a license from the NOAA Fisheries Service is required. If the business involves the facilitation or transportation of cargo by sea, a license from the Federal Maritime Commission is required. The Bureau of Ocean Energy Management, Regulation, and Enforcement must issue permission before drilling for minerals, oil, or natural gas on federal land. If the company intends to produce commercial nuclear energy, a license from the US Nuclear Regulatory Commission is required. If the business involves the disposal and distribution of nuclear materials, as well as the construction of a fuel cycle facility, a license must also be obtained.

The Federal Communications Commission requires a license for any company that broadcasts information via cable, satellite, wire, television, or radio. If the business requires the operation of overweight or oversized vehicles, the entrepreneur must also obtain permits. Furthermore, the company must follow the US Department of Transportation's maximum weight guidelines.

# CHAPTER SIX

# UNDERSTAND THE LAWS AND REGULATIONS IN BUSINESS

Even if the entrepreneur only intends to start a small business, he must be aware of certain laws and regulations to ensure the smooth operation of his enterprise.

In order to effectively advertise and market the company's products and services, the entrepreneur must ensure that any claims made are not misleading. Any marketing activity must adhere to the rules of the law. The Federal Trade Commission regulates and oversees marketing and advertising laws in the United States of America.

Such laws cover product labeling, the process of conducting telemarketing and email campaigns, environmental and health claims, and advertising to children. The commission has guidelines for marketing and advertising claims that are true. It also has compliance guides for clothing manufacturers, real estate, and franchises, among other industries. In addition, the commission is the agency to contact for telemarketing and email campaigns.

If the business intends to hire workers, the owner must follow all applicable employment and labor laws. Workers' compensation regulations, wage and hour laws, workplace poster standards, and workplace harassment and discrimination prevention are only a few of the topics covered by these laws.

The US Department of Labor is in charge of enforcing such laws, though individual states may enact their own. As a result, the entrepreneur must be familiar with federal and state employment laws.

Various financial laws exist to protect the interests of investors and small businesses. Antitrust laws promote consumer protection as well as vigorous competition from unfair business practices and anticompetitive mergers. There is also a bankruptcy law in place that must be followed. A company that sells publicly traded securities must also meet certain reporting and financial obligations. An invention, a business name, a logo, or a brilliant idea are all protected by intellectual property law. Before any entity or business person can file for copyrights, trademarks, or patents, certain procedures must be followed. To protect his business, the entrepreneur must understand this law.

There are various laws that protect the conduct of online trades for entrepreneurs who have online businesses. In the United States of America, a company can only collect sales tax from customers if it has a physical presence in a particular state. Otherwise, it will be unable to collect sales tax. If the company does not have a physical presence in the state where the customer resides, it cannot collect sales tax from those customers.

As a result, because they have no physical presence in a particular state, online retailers are unable to collect sales tax. Furthermore, sales tax is not levied in Oregon, New Hampshire, Montana, Hawaii,

Delaware, or Alaska. Some states also have tax exemptions on certain items. The entrepreneur must be knowledgeable about international commerce, customer protection, customs, duties, and taxes in order to sell internationally.

In addition, rules governing privacy are in place to protect the personal information of both employees and customers. The entrepreneur is responsible for the proper disposal of sensitive information as a business owner. It is also his responsibility if sensitive information is discarded carelessly. The Federal Trade Commission is in charge of ensuring that privacy policies and laws are followed. As a result, the entrepreneur must ensure that he or she follows the commission's guidelines for the protection of sensitive information.

The entrepreneur must also research environmental laws that may have an impact on his business. Environmental laws are properly enforced by state agencies and the Environmental Protection Agency. The business owner can research laws that may affect his company.

Borrowing money, entering into a contract, leasing equipment, and selling products and services outside of the company's state are all examples of business transactions that must adhere to the Uniform Commercial Code, which includes uniform regulations required to simplify and coordinate the sale of products as well as other business transactions. If the entrepreneur owns a small business, the Uniform Commercial Code will apply.

If he wants to take out a loan from outside the state or negotiate a lien, Code may have an impact on his business. If he wants to borrow money, he must first learn about the UCC-1 form from his prospective lender. In the case of liens, he can use the Uniform Commercial Code to secure the debtor's payment. He can learn more about the Uniform Commercial Code by visiting his state's website.

It is also critical to provide employees with a healthy and safe working environment. By law, employers must offer a secure working environment for their employees. The entrepreneur can find information about employee health and safety on the website of the US Department of Labor's Occupational Safety and Health Administration. Furthermore, the

Immigration and Nationality Act specifies nondiscrimination, employment verification, and employment eligibility requirements that small business owners must follow if they want to hire employees.

## BUSINESS STRATEGY

### What Revenue Model Will You Use?

A revenue model describes how your company will produce and deliver goods and services, generate revenue, and generate a return on investment. Long-term projections and profit potential will be heavily influenced by your revenue model.

Let's take a quick look at some of the most popular business models. As you read through these examples, consider which of these models will be most appropriate for your product/service and target market while also generating solid sales and revenues for your new company. Which model is best suited to the ownership lifestyle you seek?

**Owner/Landlord model**

In this model, a company charges a fee for the temporary use of its assets. These assets can be of a physical nature (renting an apartment to live in), a virtual nature (storing data in a cloud system online server such as Dropbox), or intellectual property (officially licensed Disney character toys). Other examples include SAAS (software as a subscription service) companies, billboard advertising, and advertising space on internet services such as Google+ or Facebook platforms.

## Creator Mode

This type of business model is for inventors, tinkerers, artists, and writers. These companies create a better mousetrap or modify existing products and services to make them better, more efficient, more appealing, and so on. These companies can also develop completely new and innovative products and services. Creator model companies can make large profits from products and services that are new enough to have little or no competition, and creator model companies can also develop products that are so innovative that the market is not yet ready for them. Even though creator model companies can sometimes vastly improve an existing product and make huge profits from a hungry market, they can also fall into the trap of creating products and services that the market does not really need. Because of these common extremes in the performance of creator model businesses, they are frequently regarded as a risky business type. According to the adage, creator model businesses are either on the cutting edge or on the bleeding edge.

**Manufacturing Model**

A manufacturer model business takes raw materials, changes their form, and produces a finished good that can be sold to consumers or businesses in large quantities. Manufacturing model companies include naming a few, the assembly line, skilled artisan, metal fabrication, packaging and labeling, machining, and construction. In this model, the products are frequently ordered to specifications by another entity, so the company or individual who orders the products bears a large portion of the risk associated with the development of new or untested products.

**Wholesaler/ Distributor Model**

This is a typical "middle-man" business model exemplified by companies that buy goods or services in bulk and then resell them to other retail businesses for a higher price than they paid for the products. Often, the main service provided by the wholesaler or distributor model business is gathering relevant products and then making those products easily accessible to retail businesses. This model can be seen in the produce industry, auto parts industry, electronics industry, and a variety of commodity-related industries, to name a few. Most industries have an extensive distribution network of wholesalers/distributors that facilitate the movement of goods between supply chains.

**Retail Model**

The retail model is well-known to the majority of consumers. Retail businesses range from Wal-Mart and Home Depot to the corner mom-and-pop shop. Every time you buy something for yourself or your family, you are most likely doing so from a retail establishment. Typically, retailers obtain their goods from distributors, directly from manufacturers, or through affiliate relationships. Some retailer-style businesses get creative by buying used merchandise, refurbishing it, and reselling it at a profit. There are numerous Amazon and eBay stores that use this method of reselling used products, as well as numerous other examples of stores that source products through more traditional channels and resell them on online platforms.

## Brokerage Model

Broker model businesses earn a commission by selling a product or service created by another business. Amazon and eBay are prime examples of online broker model businesses. They serve as a link between businesses that have products and consumers or other businesses that want the products. Broker firms receive a fee or a percentage of the sale price in exchange for that bridge. Real estate, financial advising, auction markets, and search engines are other examples of broker model businesses. The brokerage model is also used in many joint venture business relationships. In a joint venture, one company promotes the products or services of another company to its existing customer base.

**Subscription Model**

This model is used by newspapers, magazines, coffee of the month clubs, book clubs, Netflix, and many other digital marketers and information providers. Customers typically pay a monthly fee in exchange for access to products that the business produces on a regular basis, information that the business brokers, or intellectual property that the business owns. This model clearly has many components in common with the owner/landlord model and the brokerage model.

**OTHER BUSINESS MODELS**

There are numerous other business models, each with a combination of the above-mentioned characteristics and some with completely unique properties. In a book like this, it is impossible to explain every possible business model.

We have concentrated our efforts on the most common models that are most likely to suit the new venture you are launching. Manufacturer direct to consumer outlet models, business to business (B2B) models, business direct to consumer (B2C) models, franchise or licensing models, non-profit models, cooperative models, affiliate models, and multi-level or direct marketing models are examples of other types of business models.

## Who Are Your Competitors?

We've all heard the famous quote from the film The Godfather, "keep your friends close and your enemies closer." We're not suggesting you become a gangster and hatch a Machiavellian plot to eliminate your competition, but this quote can help you decide which niche to focus on within your target market.

"You will always win if you understand both your adversary and yourself," according to Sun-Tzu in *The Art of War*, adding to the depth of understanding. As a business owner, you must be aware of your competitors' capabilities, the niches they serve, their target market, how effective their solutions are, where they fall short, and their weaknesses and vulnerabilities. If you can identify a niche or segment of your common target market that the competition is ignoring or undeserving, you've found a niche market waiting to be exploited.

Spend some time now learning about your competitors and how they operate in your target market. What is their track record? Is it true that their products and services work? How well? How do they treat their clients? When researching competitors, keep in mind big box retail stores, small businesses down the street, and even online retailers.

Based on your research, list the top 5 companies you consider your competitors:

1. _____
2. _____
3. _____
4. _____
5. _____

Which of these companies serve a niche similar to the niche you will target?

_____

Describe any gaps you can find in the marketplace and how you will fill them with your product or service:

_____

_____

_____

_____

What is the secret to your competitor's success?

_____

_____

Can you improve upon their secret and make it your own?_____.

If so, how?_____

In what areas do you think your competitors are struggling?

_____

_____

How can you take advantage of these areas?

_____

Your business's unique selling point is what sets you apart from these other businesses in the marketplace.

_____

_____

_____

You don't have to come up with an entirely new concept or a game-changing invention in order to succeed. Simply put, your product or service must be simpler, better, different, faster, higher quality, easier, more efficient, or a standout solution that is distinct from what your competitors are offering. Even if the only difference between your product and the competition's is the more efficient way you tell your target market about it, that is a competitive advantage that can help your business succeed. (After that, we'll talk about how to market your new business.)

Most importantly, don't be too concerned with what your competitors are doing. Instead, concentrate on making your customers' lives easier. Treat every prospect and first-time customer as if they are destined to be a lifelong customer. You will have the repeat business and referral business you need for a thriving and successful business as you improve their lives with the products and services you offer.

TIP: While staying aware of what your competitors are doing, devote the majority of your time and energy to things you can control, such as providing better service to your customers!

Day 2 should have seen the completion of the following tasks:

- Selected Revenue Model
- How you can Set Your Product or Service Apart
- Identified competitors

**Marketing Plans**

Trying to market your product or service without a strategy is akin to hurling a can of paint at a canvas and expecting Monet to emerge. Your marketing strategy will most likely evolve over time, but for the time being, you must have a basic understanding of what you hope to achieve with your marketing efforts. The sections that follow include some tried-and-true marketing principles that will assist you in getting your solution, products and services, and new business in front of the customers who will benefit the most.

**How Will Your Prospects Find You in Sales and Marketing?**

You could have the best product in the world, but if those who need it can't find it, it's useless. How are you going to contact your customer? How are you going to get your solution in front of them? If you know your target audience and specialty, people will perceive your solution as a response to their problems or frustrations when they see it. The most important aspect of creating a successful business marketing plan is knowing how to entice them to look at your solution.

You now have a good idea of who your prospective customer is after carefully defining your niche and target market. Knowing your ideal customer means you don't have to reach out to everyone; you just have to reach out to that one person. Pay attention to the types of advertising that appear on specific channels and during specific programs, for example, the next time you're watching TV. When you watch

Monday Night Football, you will see advertisements aimed at young to middle-aged men who enjoy sports. When you watch 60 Minutes, you will see advertisements for luxury automobiles and Viagra aimed at people aged 40 to 70. If you watch Lifetime TV, you will notice advertisements aimed at women. When you watch a NASCAR race, you will see advertisements aimed at people who enjoy fast cars.

Determine the best strategies to get your product or service in front of individuals who are most likely to acquire it and become your customers as part of designing your marketing strategy. This process is both the art and science of marketing; however, marketing is more than just knowing where and how to advertise a product or service to potential customers. Marketing and marketing strategy have been the subject of numerous books. The most frequent marketing techniques and strategies that you should be aware of before beginning a marketing campaign will be briefly discussed for the sake of conciseness.

Whatever marketing tactics you use, the most important thing to remember is that if you try to promote your solution to "everyone," you will reach no one! Remember to stay focused on the niche you've identified, and nearly all of your marketing dollars should be directed solely at that one niche. It is difficult to resist the temptation to market to similar target markets or even to throw a blanket advertisement out into the wind and see what happens. When that temptation arises, remember that only large corporations with large advertising budgets, such as Coca-Cola, Apple, and Wal-Mart, can afford such broad advertisements, and even they rarely use such tactics without also running a targeted advertising campaign.

One of the most dramatic examples of this erroneous marketing is a 30-second TV spot during the Super Bowl. Yes, a lot of people will see your ad, but 97-99 percent of those people aren't ideal prospects, and none of them are ready to buy from you. Even if you could afford such an advertisement, you would have squandered a large portion of your funds. Always err on the side of targeted marketing rather than broad-based maximum exposure marketing. You will end up marketing to no one if you try to market to everyone, whereas focused marketing is always less expensive and more effective in the long run.

## Where are Your Customers Located?

Consider your ideal customer to be the most attractive man or woman you've ever seen. This individual is also your ideal soul mate in every way. You would undoubtedly want to introduce yourself to that person (pretend you're single, just in case), and you would undoubtedly want to be present where that person will be. If your ideal match is a music fan, you could look for them at local concerts. If your soul mate were very athletic, you would go to every sporting event you could in the hopes of meeting him or her. You would not look for a music lover or an athlete in a sporting goods store or an eclectic vinyl records shop. Both locations are likely to have the same outcome: You'll spend a lot of time searching for your match in the Beatles' Greatest Hits while your perfect match is busy playing the game!

Where does your intended audience congregate? Consider both physical and virtual locations that your prospective customer might visit. What is their preferred website? Is it Facebook or LinkedIn where they spend the most time? Perhaps Pinterest is their preferred social media platform. Do they frequent bars, or are they more likely to be found at a wine tasting? Would you run into them at the community center's Bingo night, or are you more likely to find them in the baby food aisle of your local grocery store? When you know where your ideal customer is likely to be, you can direct your advertising dollars accordingly.

This is not to say that someone who enjoys football would not enjoy classic rock. There are frequently overlaps in terms of what and where your ideal customer is interested in. Realistically, you're looking for a collection of things and places that will pique your customer's interest and bring the two of you together. Nonetheless, you want to narrow those overlap areas as much as possible so that you can target that prospect as precisely as possible.

How do you know what your potential customers like and where they'll go next? Simple. Inquire! You have undoubtedly encountered a few people who see what you are doing and immediately fall in love with the concept. These individuals are almost certainly part of your target market. If you don't have an easy connection to these people, go find them. Inquire about what they did over the weekend and where they went on vacation this summer. Inquire about their favorite foods and recent movies or TV shows. Learn everything you can about them. When you notice a pattern in which many of your potential customers are interested in the same things, you have reached a consensus that will allow you to focus your advertising dollars more effectively.

Consider using a blog or a Facebook page to find more areas of common interest among potential customers. Make it a habit to ask readers of your product's blog or Facebook page what kinds of things they like in a specific area on a regular basis. For example, ask them what their favorite chain restaurant is one week and then ask them to vote for their favorite song the next. When you ask questions in a friendly manner and spread them out over a period of days or weeks, your reader may not realize they are participating in a survey. To avoid misunderstandings with your customers, it is better to show that you are interested in their individuality rather than their group. Meanwhile, the trends revealed by the responses to such questions may open up a whole new channel for reaching out to potential customers.

List all of the locations where your prospective customers congregate, with a focus on the majority of your customers rather than small segments or individuals. Why do they congregate there? How often do you think you'll see them in these physical or virtual locations? What are the greatest ways to draw in customers at these locations?

**Stand Out in Your Market**

You've probably heard the expression "finding a needle in a haystack." You don't want your product or service to be that needle in the haystack. Your product or service must stand out in order for customers to notice it among the busy and crowded mass of marketing they see every day.

To make their products stand out, businesses will frequently try to show potential customers how their products are superior to similar products from other companies. Even if your product is 20%, 30%, or 50% better than a competitor's product, it is unlikely that a potential customer will notice the difference even if you point it out to them.

We live in a "better and newer" world. In modern society, the tactic of "better than" has become so overused that it is nearly meaningless. Instead, concentrate on explaining how your product or service differs from the competition. When you highlight the differences between your product and the competition's, a potential customer is much more likely to notice and recognize those differences.

Assume you are given two can openers. One can opener is made of 50% stronger plastic than the other, making it less likely to break. Could you tell which one was more powerful just by looking at them? Most likely not. It would take a lot of testing to establish which plastic was stronger. Assume the same person handed you two can openers again. For the first time, there are two options: one is a boring gray, while the other has a bottle opener attached to one end. Can you tell the difference between the two? Yes, very easily with just a glance. These are the kinds of distinctions you want to emphasize in your products. Make the distinctions clear and understandable to your customer.

What differences can you find in your product or service that will set it apart from the competition for your customer?

_____

_____

How can you alert your customer to these differences?

_____

_____

Are these differences compelling enough to make your customer choose your product over your competition's product?

___

## Speak to Your Target Market

Knowing the niche in which the majority of your potential customers reside is insufficient. You should then subdivide that niche even further into smaller groups that have some things in common but may not have everything in common with the entire niche market. The better you can segment your potential customers, the better you will be able to speak to them in a voice and on a level that will capture their attention.

Assume your business will provide the service of cleaning residential heating ducts. You've identified a market niche of people who have breathing issues because they're more likely to want their ducts cleaned. Customers in that niche will still have diverse backgrounds, interests, and activities that they participate in on a regular basis. If you identify your ideal customer as a soccer mom whose children have asthma and want your marketing to really connect with her, you should speak to her differently than you would to an empty-nester couple who are clean freaks. You could tell the mother how frightening it is for a child to have an asthma attack, while you could tell the older couple about the dust mite colonies that are growing in their air vents.

By further segmenting your target market and speaking directly to them, you can more effectively tap into their fears and desires. This type of targeted communication will aid in converting prospective customers into loyal customers.

List some ways you can further segment your target market.

_____

_____

How would you speak differently to these different groups?

_____

_____

**Market Testing**

Some of these assumptions may be related to your target market and how you identify them. Other assumptions may be more closely related to how your intended advertising methods will reach your target market. As previously stated, marketing is both an art and a science. Market testing is a scientific method of determining, early in the launch process, whether the market you selected is truly responsive to the advertising and products you are offering.

Market testing entails presenting a small-scale version of your business idea to potential customers and then receiving feedback on how they react to it. By creating a small-scale model of your marketing strategy, you can demonstrate its effectiveness before investing time and money in a full-scale version. You can also choose which of two or more possible advertising strategies will be the most effective. A/B testing is another name for this type of testing.

Consider buying some low-cost Google or Facebook ads and then creating A/B comparison landing pages. You can use Google Analytics to determine which ads sent to which markets are the most effective at getting a click-through response by sending traffic from each of several different ads to different landing pages. Begin by targeting the markets on which your marketing assumptions are based, and then fine-tune your assumptions and markets based on the data from your test.

Because not all products or services lend themselves well to A/B testing via Google or Facebook ads, you may need to get creative in order to test the responsiveness of your target market.

List at least 3 methods you will use to test your market assumptions?

1._____

2._____

3._____

**Be Consistent**

After you've tested your market and determined what types of advertisements work best, consistency and frequency are the next two most important factors in advertising success.

Marketing mediums are the means by which your advertisement is delivered to your customers.

Television, newspapers, billboards, radio, and magazines are examples of traditional marketing mediums. While traditional marketing mediums are still a viable option for advertising, their prominence has waned as newer digital and social marketing mediums have gained traction. Digital marketing allows for real-time customer engagement and is typically less expensive than traditional marketing tools, making it more appealing to small-budget startups. Look for marketing methods and mediums that you can afford to use on a regular basis to keep your product or service in front of your customers' eyes on a regular basis. If the advertising mediums you've chosen are too expensive to use on a regular basis, think about changing your strategy and finding other ways to reach your customers.

# CHAPTER SEVEN

# FINANCING YOUR BUSINESS

To ensure the success of his business, an entrepreneur must understand its financing requirements. During the business planning process, he should already know how much money he will need to start the business. At each stage of the business's development, each business' cash requirements are unique. As a result, there is no universal method for calculating business costs. Some enterprises can be started with a small amount of capital. There are also businesses that require a large sum of money to invest in equipment or inventory. Additionally, the cost of purchasing or renovating an office building, as well as the purchase of equipment, must be considered.

The entrepreneur must know how much money he will need to start his business. There are some expenses that are ongoing costs, and others that are one-time costs. Because he needs to create a realistic budget for the business, the business owner must learn how to determine whether a cost is optional or necessary. Variable or fixed expenses can be incurred for essential expenses. Commissions, packaging and shipping costs, inventory, and other costs associated with the direct sale of the service or product are examples of variable expenses. Insurance premiums, administrative costs, utilities, and rent are examples of fixed expenses.

A person's personal finances can be severely stretched when he or she launches a business. It may take years for a new business to turn a profit. As a result, it is critical for the entrepreneur to first get his finances in order before considering starting a business. A potential business owner can make a budget and commit to sticking to it. Any issues with the personal budget can cause issues with the business. Good personal credit history is also required so that suppliers and creditors can approve the business's credit terms.

**Financial Statements: An Introduction**

An entrepreneur must also understand financial statements because they can serve as a road map to avoid costly breakdowns. The balance sheet summarizes the financials of the business, including assets, liabilities, and net value. The business owner must examine the balance sheet and how it changes over time in order to determine how well his business is doing. Furthermore, it will give balance sheet readers an idea of how the business manages its inventory and collects its revenues. The income statement, on the other hand, lists all of the revenue and expenses for a given period of time. The cash flow analysis informs the reader about how money enters and exits the business. It demonstrates how well the business manages its funds. The breakeven analysis determines the point at which the business can begin to profit. An entrepreneur must determine his startup costs in order to determine how much revenue he needs to generate in order for the business to cover all of its expenses.

**Different Types of Business Financing**

An entrepreneur may require additional funding to run his or her business. Obtaining a loan is difficult. As a result, before applying for a loan, the business owner should first try to understand how his creditor will evaluate his loan application. There are two types of loans: debt financing and equity financing. If an entrepreneur wants to obtain financing, he must first determine his debt-to-equity ratio. A loan is easier to obtain if the business owner has invested more money in the business. It is best to apply for debt financing if the business' debt-to-equity ratio is low. If the ratio is too high, the entrepreneur can apply for equity financing.

The process of raising capital in exchange for shares of a business's stock is known as equity financing. In effect, the entrepreneur is granting the creditor permission to invest in his business. The creditor transforms into an investor. Many small businesses rely on equity financing. Debt financing, on the other hand, allows for capital infusion via debt instruments that must be paid with interest and the principal at the end of the loan term. The creditor is not made a stockholder in the business. The majority of business loans are secured by some sort of business asset. Commercial finance companies, credit unions, savings and loans, and banks all offer loans. Loans from friends and family members can also be obtained by the entrepreneur.

**Providing Evidence of Ability to Repay a Loan**

Before the loan is approved, the entrepreneur must demonstrate his ability to repay the loan. Most banks demand collateral as well as a cash flow from the business. Creditors examine historical financial statements. In general, banks prefer companies that have been in business for a few years. They also prefer borrowers with a track record. The loan will be approved if the entrepreneur can demonstrate that his business is consistently profitable. If the business is in its early stages or is just getting started, the entrepreneur must thoroughly explain how he intends to repay the loan.

Furthermore, the lender investigates both the business and the entrepreneur's credit histories. As a result, before applying for a loan, the entrepreneur must first check his credit report. Experian, Equifax, or TransUnion can provide him with his personal credit report. This should be the very first step. The entrepreneur must review his credit report for any errors. It takes about a month to correct the errors. As a result, the business owner must set aside enough time for this before applying for a loan.

Financing for a new business is difficult to come by. Lenders want to know that the business will be able to repay its loans, so they look at the business' equity. Equity can be increased by adding more cash from investors or entrepreneurs or by retaining earnings. Financial institutions prefer that total debts or liabilities do not exceed four times the amount of equity. As a result, if the business applies for a loan, the entrepreneur must ensure that it has enough equity to leverage the loan. Typically, he must invest more money in his business in order for the loan to be approved. Most banks will only approve up to 80% of the total loan amount.

To ensure that their money is returned, all lenders will require some form of security. As a result, they often demand collateral, which might be a business or personal asset that the lender can sell if the borrower fails to meet his loan commitments. If a borrower lacks collateral, he must seek a co-maker for the loan. This individual must have collateral that can be used as a pledge. Lenders usually will not approve a loan if there is no collateral. The collateral's value is discounted to account for the amount that will be lost if it is liquidated.

Managerial expertise is also considered by financial institutions. Creditors scrutinize the entrepreneur's experience and education because they believe that poor management is the primary cause of business failure. As a result, if an entrepreneur wants his loan approved, he must first ensure that he has strengthened his management skills.

# CHAPTER EIGHT

# PAYING TAXES FOR YOUR BUSINESS

Every activity has its own set of tax rules. No tax will be levied if the activity is merely a hobby with no intention of profit. However, if it is a business, it will almost certainly be taxed. According to the Internal Revenue Service, incorrect deduction of hobby expenses accounts for approximately $30 billion per year, including incorrect application of credits, exemptions, deductions, and overstated adjustments.

A taxpayer may deduct necessary and ordinary expenses incurred in the course of his business or trading activities. An essential expense is one that is required for the business, whereas an ordinary expense is one that is recognized and normal in his business or trade. In general, an activity is considered a business if a profit is expected. The Internal Revenue Service presumes that an activity is for profit if the individual makes a profit from such activity in at least three of the previous five taxable years. For any horse-related activity, the person must have made a profit in at least two of the previous seven years for activities such as racing, training, showing, or breeding horses. If the activity is not considered profitable, the individual cannot deduct the activity's losses from his other income. Deductions for hobbies are itemized on Schedule A.

An entrepreneur who is starting a business must first decide on the type of business entity he wants to establish because this will affect his income tax return. The federal government requires businesses to pay employers' tax, excise tax, income tax, and self-employment tax. The taxes he pays will be determined by the type of business he chooses: sole proprietorship, corporation, Limited Liability Company, partnership, or S Corporation.

In addition, the state requires the payment of corporate or business income tax. The tax basis is determined by the type of business structure. Local governments have their own tax laws. Before registering a business, an entrepreneur must first research its tax implications. He can save money for the business and even avoid problems with tax authorities if he is knowledgeable about tax laws. Each state has its own set of rules when it comes to taxes. As a result, it is prudent for the entrepreneur to consult with his or her state tax authorities regarding income tax and other taxes.

Taxable income is calculated on the basis of a tax year, which is a yearly accounting period for reporting and keeping records of income and expenses. A fiscal year or a calendar year can be used to define an accounting period. A calendar year is a year that starts on January 1 and finishes on December 31. A fiscal year is 12 months long and ends on the last day of any month other than December. The entrepreneur must keep the authorized tax year if the firm structure changes. If he wants to change it, he must first obtain permission from the Internal Revenue Service. A short tax year is one that lasts less than a year. It is used when a business does not exist for the entire year or when there is a change in the accounting period.

# CHAPTER NINE

# VARIOUS BUSINESSES YOU CAN START AS A TEEN

Entrepreneurial mindset and success do not discriminate based on age. Many successful entrepreneurs, including Mark Cuban and Fred De Luca, launched their first businesses before the age of 18. De Luca (the creator of Subway) started his first business when he was 17, whereas Cuban (the Shark Tank entrepreneur) started selling garbage bags door-to-door when he was 12. I, too, started my first business at the age of 15. As a result, the entrepreneurial spirit is not age-dependent. The following are some business ideas that you can start as a teenager.

# CLEANING AND MAINTENANCE BUSINESSES

## Lawn Care Business

Consider starting a lawn care business if you enjoy working outside and have an entrepreneurial spirit. This is a common option for teenagers to supplement their income throughout the summer. Although purchasing your own lawn care equipment can be costly, starting out with the family lawnmower is a viable option. If you don't already have any equipment, expect to spend around $3000 to get started. If you eventually grow your business to full-time status, you can earn up to $50,000 per year. Offering services like trimming, aerating, and fertilizing can help you stand out from the crowd.

**Cleaning Business**

A cleaning business comes in second on our list of business ideas for teenagers. Anyone with a keen eye for detail and a strong work ethic can succeed in the cleaning industry. You should also be physically healthy and capable of performing heavy manual tasks on a daily basis. You'll be putting in long hours and connecting with a diverse group of people, so enthusiasm and strong customer service skills will be useful.

The smallest cleaning companies are run by a single person. You can easily build a solid reputation by starting small, working on weekends or after school. This part-time hobby has the potential to grow into a full-time job over time. Larger operations employ employees or subcontractors. Some companies franchise their business model and charge franchise fees. As a result, earning potential can range from $50,000 to millions of dollars per year.

## LIFESTYLE BUSINESSES

### Babysitting Business

Babysitting is a $5 billion-a-year industry, making it an excellent choice for responsible teenagers who enjoy working with children. Finding trustworthy and dependable childcare options can be difficult for parents. They are more likely to keep and inform their friends about this great resource if they do so. This business is also extremely adaptable and simple to run regardless of your schedule.

Startup and maintenance costs are kept to a minimum, allowing profits to be maximized.

Babysitters in the United States charge an average of $13.97 per hour, with a significant geographical variation. While most businesses will remain small, one-person operations, it is entirely possible to grow your business over time by assisting clients in matching them with well-vetted babysitters in their area.

**House-Sitting Business**

Any respectable youngster wishing to help others while earning money might consider starting a house-sitting business. Housesitters should be able to care for a wide range of pets. The success of your house-sitting business will be determined largely by the reputation you are able to establish and subsequent word-of-mouth recommendations, but the potential for growth is high.

The number of clients and the consistency with which work is performed determines earning potential. This might be a wonderful weekend and holiday business when you're initially starting out. This can be a very profitable business if you can count on repeat customers throughout the year.

**Pet-Sitting Business**

Pet-sitting is a great business idea for responsible animal lovers who want to make money doing something they enjoy. As an alternative to kenneling, pet-sitters can provide a variety of services such as walks, drop-by feeding, and in-home care.

Costs are low because most pet-sitting businesses are run from the owner's home. When first starting out, word-of-mouth advertising can be extremely effective. While you're likely to start small, this business has the potential to grow significantly over time. With such cheap expenditures, pet sitters have great income potential, with full-time independent business owners earning up to $57,000 per year.

**Dog Walking Business**

The next small business idea for teens on our list is a dog-walking service. If you are an animal lover searching for flexible employment doing something you enjoy, starting a dog-walking business can be a great alternative. Whether your goal is to generate some additional money on the side or to create a long-term business, dog walking is a satisfying and dynamic activity.

Customer service that is consistently excellent and effective advertising will be critical to your success. Because pet owners are such a large market, your company's development and earning possibilities are only limited by how many dogs you can walk each day. Dog walkers who work full-time might make up to $80,000 per year.

**Professional Organizing Business**

Being a professional organizer can be a lucrative way to earn money if you enjoy organizing or have mastered the minimalist lifestyle. You must be a compassionate, understanding person who others will feel comfortable inviting into their cluttered or disorganized homes. While it is feasible to construct a flexible schedule that works for you, meeting project deadlines is crucial.

Startup costs are low because you'll only need advertising to get started. Because this is considered a specialty, luxury service, you will be able to charge a reasonable hourly rate even if you are just starting out. As your reputation grows, this business has the potential to become a lucrative full-time job. Professional organizers can earn up to $115,000 per year with very little overhead.

## ART AND DESIGN BUSINESSES

### 3D Printing Design Business

For someone with sculpting, carving, or other modeling experience, this is a fantastic opportunity. It is also necessary to comprehend the mechanics of a 3D printer as well as the market for 3D printed products. Many 3D printed goods consumers have special needs that can only be satisfied by someone who is knowledgeable about the software.

The costs of beginning a 3D printing design firm, which starts at roughly $8,000 and includes a printer, software, and some early marketing efforts, typically include a printer, software, website, and some early marketing activities. However, designing products and having them printed by a third party is a great way to get started in this field. You'll be able to establish a reputation for yourself in the industry and grow as a writer as a result of being read. Earning potential is entirely dependent on how many contracts and products you are able to make and sell, just like in any other business.

**Graphic Design Business**

Graphic design is the development of art for publications, websites, physical products, and other mediums. This business is best suited for creative individuals. You can design logos, text, or any other type of art that you or your client can think of.

Starting out can cost as little as $2,000. You will need a computer and graphic design software such as Adobe Illustrator. Many graphic designers begin their careers by working with ad agencies or through platforms that connect freelancers with interested parties. As a student, designing logos for your school or local sports teams might help you develop a great portfolio. Clients are typically charged between $25 and $100 per hour.

**Photography Business**

Starting a photography business may be a good fit for you if you enjoy taking pictures and helping people remember important events in their lives. While you will need some technical training and practice, formal education is not required. This is an excellent business opportunity for teenagers who can photograph school and social events.

Although the initial costs may be higher (a good camera, lighting equipment, a computer, and editing software), there are virtually no ongoing costs. Budget $2,000 to $5,000 for the initial investment. As your skills advance, you may be able to cover weddings or other special events. When you reach this level, your earning potential is extremely high.

**Photo Editing Business**

If you have photography and picture editing knowledge, starting an online photo editing business can be a terrific and profitable venture. While many photo editors are also photographers, this is not required. People that are skilled at using social media might find a wide range of clients online and perform particularly well.

The initial investment is low, and it includes a computer and photo-editing software. You can easily start the business for less than $5,000 if you include a good website and some advertising. To begin, you could offer to edit photos for school or local publications in order to build your portfolio. It's feasible to expect a five-figure yearly pay if you continue to build your business, with the potential to exceed $100,000 per year.

**Illustration Business**

A successful illustration business is an excellent way for talented and artistic teenagers to earn money. Some possible careers include book illustration, cartoon character creation, and storyboard design. Maintaining current knowledge of digital illustration technologies is also essential in this industry.

The costs of starting an illustration business are low, as are the costs of art supplies and artistic computer software. Begin by creating illustrations for school newspapers, local publications, or special gifts for friends and family. Your earning potential will grow in tandem with your portfolio and reputation. Professional illustrators earn an average of $55,000 per year, but specializing in a specific market can help you reach a six-figure salary.

## Makeup Artist Business

As a makeup artist, anyone who enjoys dealing with people and has outstanding makeup application skills may find success. Using social media to make a name for oneself may be really advantageous.

To begin, you can build your portfolio by doing makeup for friends at events such as prom. As a teenager, this is an excellent business to start. Your customers will return for special occasions for the rest of their life if you develop a reputation among your peers early on. Because most makeup artists work from home or travel to their clients, startup costs are relatively low. As your business expands, you can earn a sizable profit, with the most successful makeup artists earning six figures.

## WRITING AND PUBLISHING BUSINESSES

### Freelance Writing Business

Teens can find a plethora of freelance writing opportunities. With the internet's ever-expanding reach, businesses are publishing more content in an effort to reach audiences worldwide from a variety of perspectives. Anyone interested in pursuing a writing career should take advantage of this opportunity to start constructing a portfolio.

Aside from the cost of your computer, Wi-Fi, and advertising, the startup and maintenance costs are virtually non-existent. Earning potential is good due to low costs and high growth potential for those who can find consistent or long-term clients. Established freelance writers can earn between $30,000 and $50,000 per year.

**Transcription Business**

This business is ideal for teenagers who need to work around their hectic school and extracurricular schedules. You will spend most of your time transcribing audio or video that has been provided to you. Those who can type swiftly, pay close attention to detail, and are familiar with computers and other associated software and technology are also good candidates for the position.

Although startup costs are low, the growth potential of a transcription business varies greatly by industry. Medical transcription, for example, has grown rapidly over the last decade. However, regardless of the subject matter, if you provide quick and accurate work, you can build a successful transcription business. Because many transcription projects are billed by the project, your speed and accuracy will also play a significant role in determining your earning potential. The more quickly you work, the more money you can make.

**Data Entry Business**

Data entry businesses are ideal for detail-oriented individuals who are familiar with spreadsheet and word processing software. Because flexible part-time data entry work is available, this business can accommodate a student's busy schedule while providing valuable work experience.

Startup costs are minimal, with only your computer required to get your business up and running. A small business with only one or two staff will often take on a few clients and develop long-term connections with them, making this an excellent business to grow as you advance from student to professional.

**Children's Book Business**

Starting a children's book business may be a good fit if you enjoy writing, drawing, or telling stories. Due to the amount of reading done by children versus adults, children's books have regularly sold more copies than adult novels.

Startup costs for a self-publishing individual range from $5,000 to $15,000, but with more flexible and affordable self-publishing resources appearing all the time, it's easier than ever to publish on a budget. As a result, the earning potential is very high. Children's book authors who are successful earn well over $100,000.

## SOCIAL MEDIA & ECOMMERCE BUSINESSES

### eBay Store

Self-motivated individuals who are already familiar with eBay are good candidates for this position. Knowing what sells well, how to price products appropriately, and how to get your listings noticed will help you succeed in this business. While you must ensure that your items are well-presented and that you follow up with buyers, this business can easily accommodate a busy student's schedule. It's also a business that you can tailor to your specific interests and experience, making it both enjoyable and profitable.

Only the seller's time and scope limit the seller's potential for growth. Finding a specialty or niche area where you can sell popular products that you are passionate about is a great success strategy. With low startup and maintenance costs, your earning potential is virtually limitless once you get things going.

**Social Media Marketing Business**

A social media marketing business is the next small business idea for teens on our list. Young people have grown up with social media, giving them an advantage in terms of knowing how to use and navigate all of the major platforms. If you enjoy engaging with huge groups of people and are fascinated by how social media platforms work, social media marketing could be a lucrative career for you.

Starting a social media marketing business does not have to be expensive. You can start a social media marketing business if you have access to a computer or a smartphone. Individuals and large corporations are examples of potential clients. High earners in this industry make more than $100,000 per year.

**Etsy Store**

If you enjoy making handmade goods or hunting down unique vintage items in your spare time, you might enjoy running an Etsy shop. This is a great place for young artists to sell their work, as well as anyone interested in making and selling well-made products. Sellers must have the talents necessary to locate or manufacture the things they offer, as well as basic computer skills and marketing or advertising experience to help promote them.

These fundamental skills, combined with a strong entrepreneurial spirit, can help you turn your hobby into a profitable business opportunity. While you'll most likely start small, this is a business that you can grow over time and shape to fit your schedule throughout school and beyond. Serious sellers are making six figures, so this is a fantastic opportunity to start a business that will grow with you.

**Live-Streaming Business**

Earning money while playing video games is a pipe dream for the majority of young gamers. This is something that, with enough enthusiasm and drive, can become a reality. To do so, gamers should sign up for a popular streaming site like Twitch.TV and plan to spend many hours each day streaming their games and increasing their fan following. Those who gain enough followers to become partners (500 or more on Twitch, for example) will start earning money for the traffic they generate.

Developing and maintaining a large following necessitates exceptional gaming skills. You'll also need to know how to use social media to promote yourself, respond to comments, and establish a strong online presence. The goal is to amass a large enough following to become a partner on your streaming site. Those who do so can earn thousands of dollars per month while doing something they enjoy.

## SPECIALITY CRAFT BUSINESSES

### Soap-Making Business

Those who enjoy working with their hands should consider starting a soap-making business. Making high-quality soap is a skill that anyone can learn, but it does require practice. Buying raw materials, combining and creating fragrances, making soap, and selling soap are all part of running a soap-making business.

Because the materials used to make soap are relatively inexpensive, the profit margin in a soap-making business is high. Expect to spend around $500 on soap materials and equipment to get started. If you decide to sell online, you'll also need to invest in marketing and the creation of a website. The amount of money you can make depends on the sort of soap you sell and how far you can spread your business, but the potential for growth is enormous. What begins as a small side hustle has the potential to grow into a national brand.

**Jam Business**

Anyone who enjoys cooking for others will enjoy starting a jam business. This is yet another excellent and adaptable business that a teen can start in their sparc timc.

Making jam has very low startup costs, especially if you start on a small scale. To make your first batch, you can spend less than $300 total on canning tools and ingredients. To begin, most jam companies sell their products at a local market or strange. Finding a local restaurant to carry your jam is a good way to expand your jam business. The earning potential is high, as with other specialty businesses, with full-time efforts bringing in around $1,000 per week.

Gift-Wrapping Business gift-wrapping is a terrific method to supplement your holiday income. You can set up booths near department stores or work from the convenience of your own home. This business is ideal for students because most transactions will take place on weekends and during holidays.

You should expect to spend some time and money on creating an appealing and professional-looking booth as well as purchasing supplies. However, because this business has a high-profit margin, your earning potential is high. Growing your gift-wrapping business from seasonal to year-round can be difficult, but wrapping gifts in the later months can be profitable for a short time.

## Sewing Business

A sewing business is a great method for a creative seamstress to make extra money. This business allows for a great deal of flexibility and is ideal for young people who are particularly interested in current fashion trends.

Startup costs are minimal, particularly if you already own a sewing machine. While you'll probably start small, giving simple repairs and patch-ups, students might expand their business by offering to help with custom design and building for school plays or repairing uniforms for sports teams. Your customer base and earning potential will rise as your reputation grows.

**Candle Making Business**

Anyone who is creative and crafty may be interested in starting a candle-making business. It's a fantastic way to start a business from the comfort of your own home. You can sell handmade candles to friends and family, at craft fairs or weekend markets, or online through your own Etsy store or website.

Materials are only a few hundred dollars in the beginning. How many candles you can manufacture and how much time you dedicate to selling them will decide your growth and profitability, but a conscientious candle maker can establish a fairly significant and profitable business.

## TEACHING AND COACHING BUSINESSES

## Art Lessons

Starting an art courses business can be a pleasant and fulfilling effort if you enjoy meeting and working with people and enjoy art. You will need to develop structured lessons so that your students can follow a path as they learn an artistic skill.

To start an art lessons business, you don't need much. You can either supply your own tools (brushes, pencils, paper) or require your students to provide their own. This is a great business for young people to start because it can be done from the comfort of their own home for free. You may even be able to reserve free space at your school or library. Your hourly prices will vary based on your skill level and the topic of your courses, but most instructors can charge at least $25 per hour, making this a great method to start earning and saving money.

**Home Tutoring Business**

If you excel at a particular subject in school, you should think about starting a home tutoring business. You can design your own lessons or simply assist students in completing their school assignments while ensuring that they understand the material. As a student, you are uniquely placed to identify people who require additional assistance.

Because you can tutor from the comfort of your own home or the home of your students, your startup costs are minimal. You might have to invest some time and money in advertising, but simple fliers can be quite effective if you have a captive audience of students in your school or region. Most home tutors work on a per-hour basis and assist students with a specific subject. With experience, you can charge $30-$40 per hour, making this a profitable and rewarding business.

**Test Prep Business**

Starting a test prep business can be a lucrative endeavor if you've mastered the art of standardized tests and want to share your knowledge with others. Specializing in a specific test (such as the SAT or ACT) is a good method to discover people to tutor, and you'll have no trouble getting clients if you're still in high school. Using test prep books and providing general test-taking advice are two methods for assisting struggling test-takers to improve.

This business has low startup costs, with the only expenses being the purchase of a test prep book and a website. Helping friends and classmates is a great and simple way to get started and establish a good reputation. Because performing well on tests is important to most students, test prep tutors can usually charge more per hour than regular tutors.

**Music Lessons Business**

Giving music lessons can be a lucrative source of income for a young entrepreneur. You can easily discover students that need lessons or extra help if you have a lot of expertise playing your instrument.

Music lesson business startup costs can be kept minimal, especially if students bring their own instruments. You'll need to buy some sheet music, but lessons can be held at your house, your student's house, or even at school if time allows. You'll be able to raise your rates as your reputation grows. Music teachers typically charge between $30 and $60 per hour; so this business can be very profitable over time.

# CONCLUSION

Some entrepreneurs start their businesses when they are young, and there are no rules that say you must be in your twenties or older to start a business. If you only make a few dollars per week, there aren't many advantages to starting a formal business right now. However, if you earn more than that — or if you want others to respect your job — it can be worthwhile to go a step further.

If you are too young to start your own business, your parents may be able to assist you. Why not stand out from the crowd and take your business to the next level if your state enables minors to create their own businesses?

Everyone now has access to teen entrepreneurship, thanks to the internet. You will have a good chance of success if you can come up with a great idea, carve out a niche, establish your reputation, and put together a solid business plan.

# If You Liked This, Then You'll Love

Scan this barcode or enter this link to order yours today!

https://rb.gy/52e6cx

# We Would Love Your Feedback!

Scan this barcode or follow this link to leave a review

https://rb.gy/fhhdku

Made in the USA
Las Vegas, NV
09 June 2022